The Snow Globe

By

Marisa Moris
Joseph Moris

Joseph Moris and Marisa Moris

DEDICATION

This book is dedicated to everyone with curiosity and the willingness to change their lives

The Golden Rule

Jesus says:

"Do unto others what you would have them do unto you"

&

"The snow globe example is the whole basis of my teachings for this is my teachings on the Holy Spirit"

Always be humble and gentle.

Because of your love, be patient with each other, making allowance for each other's faults.

Make every effort to keep yourselves united in the Spirit, binding you together with peace.

Marisa's Introduction to the Snow Globe

Our lives are made up of moments, snap shots in our minds of who we are, who our family is and what we mean to the world and the people around us. Most of our memories are made up of the pictures that we have seen time and time again in the family photo albums or from the pictures that hang on our parents walls. The stories that our family and friends tell over and over seem to be the things we remember most, but what about all the other times in our lives? What about the other 99.9% of our life?

Do you remember your life? Do you remember how you felt at night before bed when no one was around and no was talking to you about the day? Do you remember the things that you would think about? Do you remember how you felt about yourself and who you felt you were to the world? Do you remember what YOU wanted to be when you grew up…? Not what your parents or family wanted you to be or told you that you would be the best at?

Life is funny, it is my belief that as souls, we choose these lives, we choose our parents, we choose the town we will live in and we even choose our birthday and in most cases we help to choose our name. What if you could go back in time and share something with YOU when you were young? If you had an hour with you at any age what would you share or teach yourself? Asking myself that question I immediately knew! I would share this book, all the healing energies that the guides and I programmed into it and the simple lessons that come with it…. I would go back to when I was 7 and I would teach me The Snow Globe!!

After I channeled the first paragraph of this introduction I sat and thought about what I had written. Were my memories my own? Did I grow up living a life based on other's memories and beliefs? I can remember hanging on every last word that my aunt would share about her personal life and the lives of her friends but I never heard the other side of the story. If I had heard the other side, would I have grown up to be a different person? Probably not. Would my view and perspective on men and their inability to be trusted or depended on have been different, absolutely! Would my life have then been different? Maybe! Would I have had respect for authority and men earlier in life? Maybe, but that is not the point. The point I am trying to make is, how many of your memories are not your own and therefore how many feelings and beliefs do not belong to you but effect you every single day? How many memories are shaded with the perception of the person who told you the story or the one who tells it the most? How much of other's people's opinions effect the person you are today?

I believe we are all spirts living a human experience, we are here to live and love and feel joy and peace. Over the last 5 years I have personally done medical intuitive healing, spiritual counseling, and angelic reading sessions on over 10,000 people and out of those 10,000 people I would say maybe 10 of them claim to remember a majority of their childhood to present day, why do you think that is? Can you remember back to when you were 11 years old and recall the entire day? I bet you can't and either can I because it's not really important what we have done but it is important how we have felt while doing it. That is why we only remember and talk about the emotional times in our lives, and that is why healing our emotions or the pieces of us that are traumatized by emotional times is extremely important.

However, regardless of its importance, no one looks forward to dredging up the past and talking about something that makes them feel bad so in most cases we just ignore the feelings, or try to forget them by bottling them up inside. I will go as far as to say that up until 10 years ago that bottling things was sometimes the easiest route because it didn't cause the damage it almost immediately causes today.

The world is a different place, the vibration of the ethers are different and our emotions if not dealt with and cleared quickly, are killing people, causing us to get attachments that cause mental illness, and the guilt, shame, fear, and depression that we had 30 years ago and never released are showing up as tumors, Alzheimer's, seizures, cancers, limes disease, rheumatoid arthritis to name a few. In the 8 years I have been doing healing I can say with 100% confidence that EVERY PHYSICAL ailment starts with an emotional issue that has gone unattended.

I am super excited about this book because although I have now been part of over 15 published books there is nothing that I feel so personally connected to and protective of as the snow globe. It came at a time in my life when I should have been happy, I should have been at peace but of course, because of my personal behavior patterns, I was criticizing myself, putting myself down and living in a state of worry, fear, and "I am not worthy" even though I had begun to meditate, communicate with my angels, and had been successful in working a pretty good spiritual practice of self-awareness whereby I was able to look at myself "in the mirror", call myself on my own stuff, and begin making changes in my life.

Christmas 2011 I was at my friend Kimba's house at a group meditation that I had put together so that my mediumship teacher could teach us all about connecting to spirits and giving readings. Before the lesson each week he would lead a 15 minute meditation to get everyone into the right frame of mind to learn and be open to the spirit world. Each week he would lead us to into a big ball of light and into a land where we would be led to meet our guide and every week most of the people in the class would have AMAZING experiences and report back with detailed stories of what and who their guide was and the adventures they had been on while I was struggling to sit still through the 15 minute meditation while staring at the back of my black eyelids and obsessing about how much I sucked at meditation! I never met a guide, I couldn't even conceptualize going on an adventure because I logically KNEW I was in Kimba's living room, the whole thing was stupid to me but I wanted to meet my guide and wanted to learn to communicate with the spirits I was now seeing. I began to get desperate and depressed because my logical mind started to convince me that I was wasting my time with all this spiritual stuff I had grown to enjoy studying so much!

Then one night right before Christmas I finally met my guide…. As we were being led into the ball of light I started to be able to make out the silhouette of a man. He was in all white, with fur around his collar and the bottom of his robe. He was holding a staff and had a BIG white beard and long white wavy hair. It was SANTA! Not the fat Santa that wears red, but the one that wears white and is all trim and wise looking. My mind went into so many places... from REALLY?! My freaking guide is Santa?! Is this metaphoric for how "real" guides are? Is this a joke? to OH WOW I LOVE Santa, how exciting to have him as my guide!

"Santa" walked up to me and said "I know you are sad, we hear your cries, please don't hurt yourself anymore, it hurts us to see how much you think you hate yourself" then he reached out his hand that seemed to grow into the size of the room and in his hand he had a snow globe that I was now in.

He said "You ARE a Snow globe and I have you in the palm of my hands. We love you so much and will NEVER let you go!" Then from straight above the snow globe a huge beam of light came pouring in through the glass and zapped me with so much light it was blinding. Although I literally felt like I was in a snow globe with all the colored snowflakes and dark black water swirling around me in "real life" I could feel back pain releasing, my head tingling, and my left eye started twitching. It was SUPER weird to say the least but beyond cool at the same time. I was finally experiencing, in meditation, my version of a "grand adventure" like the ones my classmates had shared in the past. I NEVER wanted to wake up and return to Kimba's house!

Then in what seemed like seconds later the mediumship teacher began to bring us back to the room and everything disappeared. I left Kimba's house that night feeling like I was 12 years old again! I was happy! I was joyous and had a new found love for my life!

About a month later my dad and I got together and I did a healing session for him. This session would lead to our weekly channelings with the guides who helped to write Answers Heaven Speaks and all the books to follow. Before doing a healing on my Christian father for the first time I was so filled with fear because I could see he was afraid that I was talking to the dark side. This scared me because I finally felt that I had found my calling and I did not want for him to think I had finally lost it and discourage me in any way from pursuing the path I was just starting on. I was finally so sure about my place and what I wanted to do in this life and didn't want anything to jeopardize that. I knew with every piece of my being I wanted to channel and I wanted to heal people.

I knew if I said a prayer to protect us that we were supposed to be protected but this time I did not feel protected after our prayer, I only felt fear. I was not sure what to do. All of a sudden I heard in my head "You are a snow globe and you are in the palm of my hands" and the whole house, in mind's eye, turned into a snow globe then a shower of white light came pouring down over the "snow globe". I felt peace and so much joy! The session went amazingly well and we are here today writing books because of it.

In February of 2012 the guides came through with some teachings about the snow globe. The long channeled message that is in the next chapter was brought through to me and my dad. They explained what the snow globe is and it made so much sense. Since then we have both used the snow globe in our own way every single day.

This little book is going to change the way you see your life. Whether you are filled with your family's snowflakes (beliefs) that are not even your own and because of that you are not attracting the things into your life that you REALLY want or you are attached to another person's snow globe and feeling stuck in the past even though your mind is ready to move on you are going to see that the snow globe exercise will fix all of that. The only requirement is a desire for change! In fact, you don't even need to know that you want change, nor do you need to know what or if there is an issue at all. You just need a willingness to devote 5 minutes to YOU each day and the ability to imagine in your mind what a snow globe looks like and a bright light above it.

The snow globe has become the center of all my spiritual teachings and the most effective tool in teaching my students to become clairvoyant (to see energy) and clairsentient (to feel). My dad, being the "keep it simple stupid" guy that he is stuck with the basic description of the Snow Globe from 2012 and uses it every day. I of course, being the "I over complicate everything for myself because if it's difficult it must be better" have over complicated things over the years. Writing this book and bringing back the basics have been super refreshing and helpful to me! Over complicating things has however had some major benefits because through that process I have found ways of using the snow globe as a quantum healing tool. I am literally unable to teach healing, meditation, chakras, cords, soul retrieval, channeling, intuitive readings, and mediumship without first teaching the snow globe.

The following chapters are pretty much my first hour of every class I teach to my new students. Jesus is the one that channeled it because he is me and my dad's shared guide and Peter is another guide who has become our fun loving buddy who loves to come in with commentary. If I was to be channeling this same information with Bill and Gayle Gladstone (my other co-authors) the same information would have come through but it would have been Saint Germaine or Michael who spoke because they are our shared guides and in essence higher dimensional versions of Jesus (Michael is Christ or Jesus' Higher Self) and Peter (Saint Germaine and Peter share a higher self).

The point I am trying to make is that my dad is Christian so the book has a Christ like flavor however the snow globe is NOT religious in ANY way and I do not want the way it is talked about in the following conversation with the guides to defer anyone from using it. However, to all you Christians out there you can be assured that the energy we are working with is Christ light, creator energy (your individual creator soul), and the white light of unconditional love (holy spirit). I hope that you enjoy this little book, it should take no more than a couple hours to read and if you do not have time to read all about the snow globe, what it is and how it works just yet, flip to page 72 or go to www.mysnowglobe.us to watch the exercise for connecting to your higher self and protecting and clearing your energy using The Snow Globe. Make sure to write down all the things you want in life so that you can do the manifestation exercise at the end of the book after you do the initial 5-minute exercise of connecting to and clearing your "snow globe".

Have fun!

Love, Marisa

The Guides Explain the Snow Globe to Marisa and Joe

The transcribed words of Jesus channeled through Marisa in February 2012

The light within each human being is strong! The light in each human being is there and it can only be extinguished by human emotions that man has deemed as wrong.

What we would like to explain, though, is that some human beings feel that some things are wrong that are not considered wrong with other human beings. So evil and wrongs really all depend upon the consciousness and rules that that human being was brought up in. Man-made laws make up a huge difference as to what a human perceives as right or wrong. Where a person is born and what kind of a society and home life this human is brought up in makes up the psyche of what is considered right and wrong. For instance, if you are Muslim and you don't pray five times a day then you think you are evil. If you are a Christian and you don't pray five times a day, well, let's just say that doesn't compute so no that person doesn't think of this as a wrong. Some spiritual groups, like the American Indian, ritually dance and feel that brings them closer to God whereas a strict Baptist or Apostolic believes dance is the work of the devil.

The Holy Spirit, or as we call it, The Light, resides in each and every person whether they acknowledge it or not. The Light is within; the Light is pure; the Light is strong; the Light is quite astounding; The Light is within us over here as well. This is the Guiding Light. This is the Morning Star that guides us through the physicality. This is the star that leads us through the ethers and through the heavenly realms.

When the soul is damaged, hurt, when the aura has holes in it, when the body is damaged, not just the physical body, but the emotional, mental, spiritual body, and those of the subtle bodies are damaged, the Light does not necessarily get dimmer, it just makes it harder for the consciousness of the human being to see and feel the Light. What they see and feel instead is to see darkness, to see emotions, to see those things in the human field, <u>not the spiritual field.</u>

What we would like to explain to you is the Light coming from each and every Higher Self down into the physical body of that being is strong. Inside that physical being there is the Holy Spirit, the Soul. Inside that physical body, that Soul has experiences that have been carried forward from and throughout past lives.

The Soul and Holy Spirit never waver in their strength within the human body and mind. By turning over the human mind and will to God through visualization, one is opening oneself up and allowing God to shine down into the human's energy field (snow globe) and through the crown chakra of the physical body, down through the energy centers and connect with the Holy Spirit within.

See this energy field as your aura, a big globe, a "Snow Globe". The light shining from above is the God/Source beaming this intense light down into the middle of this Snow Globe. In the center of this Snow Globe is a statue and that is the human being (you). That statue inside carries the Holy Spirit. When that statue acknowledges the Light of God, the Light from Source that shines down, that guides them, that leads them each and every day, it opens them up to connect with their Holy Spirit. The Holy Spirit is ignited by this Light that shines directly down into the statue and ignites the fire within. This fire within is that burning desire that humans feel to do good; this is that tear they drop when they have done good and they know they are good.

When the "statue" experience emotions, when they experience human emotions, these human emotions cause fogging inside the snow globe. Every time that statue experiences something negative or something they "believe" is bad, colored snowflakes will be created. When one does so many things that they believe are bad those snowflakes thicken and thicken and thicken so that the light coming from above isn't as strong anymore. The Light becomes scattered. The Holy Spirit still burns within but the desire to connect with God becomes blocked by all the dark snowflakes floating around inside the snow globe. Despite the Holy Spirit still burning with the desire to do good, the fog of human emotions like guilt, anger, and despair are filling up their snow globe, so this is when depression sets in and this is when real human instinct will kick in.

Humans are creatures of instinct, just like animals. They eat, they sleep, they kill, they protect themselves, and they mate. This is what humans do. So in order to fully understand and feel the Holy

Spirit within, one needs to ask if their snow globe will be purified by the Light of Source (The IAM for Jews...Christ for Christians...Buddha for Buddhists...Brahma for Hindus) and have these emotions, the sadness, the despair and other human failings removed.

When this statue, sitting in the middle of the snow globe asks for help, this fog dissipates, is taken away and is enveloped within The Light. And, with this intense beam of light, the Holy Spirit is reignited to fill the Snow Globe with intense light which can clear out the "fog".

Typically, the interference/the fogging is caused by guilt. Humans feel guilt and guilt becomes the killer of the body and the soul. One begins life completely connected with the Light and the Holy Spirit. As they grow they may not be religious, but they are a child, they are innocent. The Light of Christ/Source/God is flowing through them igniting their Holy Spirit and this is their childhood. As they begin to age and become a part of the "world" they are hurt and told not to do that, or "you're not supposed to do this". Guilt begins to build. This guilt begins to block the connection between God and the Holy Spirit within each soul. As this child grows, this child learns rules and this child might do things that are wrong.

This may be a very dogmatic, religion-ruled household that this child is born into, and soon they will build up massive amounts of guilt, therefore blocking them from their creator. Guilt causes one to look outward at another's guilty nature. It is human-nature; it is the ego's nature, to not look at oneself for what one has done when one feels guilt. One will not look at the things that they have done, they instead will look at what others have done so that the ego feels better. Does this take away the fog? No, it deepens it because inside, the Holy Spirit, the Holy Spirit inside them, knows they are pointing fingers at others for things that they have done.

So this is the human condition that runs rampant throughout earth. This is the human condition of the ego, of the emotions. The more people that understand, the more souls that understand that each and every human being on this planet is their brother; that they are all one, the faster they will clear the fog from their snow globe, their life and each and every human being will become more and more connected, not only to themselves above, their Christ self, the Holy Spirit, their Higher Self, but they will also be connected as one because they will realize that up above they are all one. We all come from the same Source.

We bring to you this information in hopes that the remaining words in this little book will be spread throughout your society to help these human beings to clear the fog in their snow globes, their auras. Clearing these hardships, clearing these damages to the human aura will help society completely for sometimes the knowledge and the knowing that the religion that someone was brought up in, the household they were brought up in, and realizing and knowing that the words you speak that explain that, then maybe they weren't so bad, maybe these rules were man-made.

Maybe God loves them no matter what. Maybe their Higher Self had planned it this way? Maybe it's not all their fault, maybe it's their human nature, maybe it's their ego; maybe it's their emotions. This is not to blame bad behavior on the ego or emotions, but for one to completely understand that in turning their life and their will over to their Higher Self or God, or the Christ within, aka the Holy Spirit, one can begin to see their life as not being a life that is happening "to" them but a life that is in the palms of their hands. They may create the life that they desire. Life is not just happening to them.

As people begin to understand this information and they begin to see and know that there is a Light within them regardless of whom or what they believe in, as long as they can believe that there is something greater than themselves then the Light above, guiding and leading them, whether it be Christ, their Higher Self, their Soul, or Angels or Guides, does not matter as long as they believe that there is a Light greater than them, above them, guiding them and they can turn their will in life over to that higher being and the Holy Spirit will be ignited within them. This does not just have to be done within the Christian faith, this can be done in any way a human mind and ego wishes. The key here is turning the ego and the will of the emotions over to the Light on a regular basis.

What is the Snow Globe and how do I put it to work?

My dad and I were sitting in the living room getting ready to do yet another channeling session where I would go into trance and he would ask questions of Jesus, Abraham, Peter, Michael, and the rest of the "crew" that would tend to show up when we would call in the beings best suited and the safest to talk to when asking questions about universal truths and ancient knowledge. The books we were working on at the time are The Bible Speaks series which I begrudgingly agreed to do mostly to make my dad happy. Looking back, I am happy I caved in and worked on those books because everything that I know now has come from the 100's and 100's of hours that we spent talking to the so called authors of the Bible and many more including Jesus and Mary and, of courses, our Higher Selves.

My dad said that he had felt like someone was telling him to write a book about the snow globe when he was driving over and interestingly enough I had been thinking about making a little manual to teach new students how to use the snow globe to develop their abilities and heal themselves. That was all my dad had to say to get me SUPER excited!! The snow globe is the BEST thing that ever happened to me. The Snow Globe has protected me, it has helped me to teach and most importantly it has helped me to SEE energy when I could only hear it before I started working with the snow globe.

I realize this sounds crazy, however the crazier the better sometimes. When something defies all logic and the imagination is FORCED to take over this is when we can really begin to hear, see, and feel the invisible guidance that each and every human being has on this planet.

The following is the channeled session me and my dad had. Jesus is me and my dad's shared guide and pretty much the only being my dad, being a Christian, would trust throughout the creation of our books so as always he showed up to deliver the information. Peter, who was his usual goofy and fun loving, yet wisdom filled self, was there along with Mary Magdalene who didn't share much that day but explained that she came to watch. In addition to those two there here were lots of "people" from above including mine and my dad's higher selves who joined in to watch the session but for the most part, this was all Jesus.

We had been given an outline to follow in a previous session so we covered a few topics on how to use the Snow Globe and for what purposes such as relationships, work and the manifestation of the things we desire in our lives.

I AM a Snow Globe

(Snow globe recording with Jesus – April 30, 2016)

MARISA: Peter and Jesus are here…Our higher selves are here as are Adam and our highest level shared guide, Michael. Noah is here also. I think Noah is a layer of your higher self, he is saying "I am Big Joe I am also an Ascended Master."

JESUS: Yes, yes my brother, you have been doing your work, you have been doing your work and in doing this you are ascending, you are moving in line with all aspects of yourself. And for this we are very proud…But what you must understand is even by just clearing out your snow globe everyday there are things that will be missed – this is why we are so excited about this book – because although it seems simple and although it seems like things that we have already talked about before, there are things that you will soon forget because we will get into other more complicated things, and then it won't be as exciting for the two of you to put this into a new book. We want to memorialize this teaching because the snow globe will change the world…"

JOE: It's going to be simple. I use the snow globe all the time. I tell people, look, it's really simple.

MARISA: …What Jesus is saying, he says:

JESUS: What we would like to say is that the snow globe, although it is just a visualization of a common ordinary snow globe, is attached to the idea that it symbolizes your entire energy field. We do not need to be specific about which layers of the aura are in the snow globe and which layers are not in the snow globe; just where the consciousness is. We do not need to be specific about any of this. All we must do is say, today, right here, right now, set the intention that the snow globe that we speak of in here is an all-encompassing field of energy surrounding all layers of a human being. So, when someone is calling in the golden liquid Christ-light energy from above, the white light from the creator, and silver light from their Creator Self (or I am) they are clearing out all layers of their mental emotional and spiritual body. Prior to this it was set that the snow globe was just the spirit realm around the physical body we are changing it to simplify and also make the healing more effective and multidimensional in nature.

JOE: Okay, first thing is how does a person visualize the snow globe? What do they ask for from Jesus to set up their protective snow globe?

JESUS: First of all, the person does not need to ask me, Jesus, they do not need to ask anyone. They can ask Source, the Creator Self within, or the divine white light in general but all they really need is to "ask" their own mind.   Through their mind's imagination all they must do is ask to see themselves and the field around them as a snow globe. All they must do is say in their mind "I am a Snow Globe". They may imagine that they are the statue inside of this snow globe, they may imagine that the water and snowflakes are the energy in the field around the physical body and that the glass is the outside of the "personal bubble" or aura. You may imagine how far out from your body or how big your snow globe is. Some days it may be 30 feet in diameter; some days it may be two feet, some days it may be five feet. All the person must do is use their mind within their brain to imagine this snow globe around them. Once they imagine what this looks like, then they must imagine what the statue (which represents the physical body) looks or feels like. Then they may take their attention to what the snowflakes floating around the statue, with in the snow globe, feel like to them at that particular moment. Do they feel heavy? Do they feel light? Do they feel dark? Do they feel white? Does the water feel clean? Does it feel goopy; does it feel dirty? Just by them taking their attention to their mind and imagining this, what they are in fact doing is bringing their consciousness and their awareness into their human mind, into the center of the mind where the pineal gland is, and they are able to see or 'imagine' this snow globe around them. Using this technique will allow them to think that they are imagining this when in fact they are really seeing the energy on their body (statue), the snowflakes (energy) in their aura (snow globe) and the light with in them (their spirit) with their third eye. When we tell people to try to look at something with their third eye, they say, 'I cannot do that, I am not psychic and what is a third eye anyway?!" So we would like to stick with "imagine this" or "feel this". But, they must also imagine or feel the details, they must imagine what does their statue look or feel like right now? What does the glass look or feel like right now? Is it dirty, is it clean? What does it feel like? This is how they begin to imagine it or in other words "tune into their energy".

- *An alternate way of doing this exercise is to say "I am a snow globe" and imagine that there is a snow globe on a table in front of you. What does the snow globe look like? What color it? What does the statue look like? What color are the snowflakes? Is the water clean, clear, or dirty? Is it goopy? Just imagine what it looks like and as the light DIRECTY from above comes down and cleans the snow globe it will be just as effective as if you were imagining yourself in it however as you get more use to doing this imaging yourself inside will make all of the manifestation exercise and all other techniques we and this channel teach much more accurate because you will be able to see up close what is there. it will be just as accurate is if you were imagining you were in the snow globe.*

Connect to Higher Self

JOE: So, before they ask for the Christ light or Source to come into the crown chakra of the statue inside the snow globe do they also visualize that they have set up their snow globe with all the darkness and the stress and the cords and everything else that have caused them to come to ask for the snow globe or do they visualize it as clean? If they visualize it as "goopy" do they then visualize the light as it comes in so that this incoming light will blow all the darkness away? Should they picture the darkness inside their snow globe as well, prior to asking for Source to bring in the energy to blow it all away?

JESUS: "Yes, and the magical thing about this, the magical thing about the encryption, so to speak, that we're putting into this book, is that by people just imagining the snow globe around them and looking to see what their snow globe looks like in their imagination, one day they may see themselves as a horse in the middle, a beautiful decorated horse, and they may see their snow globe as being 50 feet wide and it is sparkly white, there is no muck, there is no dirt in it. Other days it may be covered in goop and there may be a tiny little gremlin statue in the middle or they may see themselves as the statue with a little gremlin on the statue. They must just allow their "imagination" to run wild so to speak. Based on what their energy is like and the way that their brain reads the energy is how they will imagine the snow globe at that particular time. So they do not need to put any dirt within it, but if they imagine the snow globe and the dirt is there it is because they have energies that need to be cleaned. With the Snow Globe visualization, we are asking the imagination to become a magical tool in healing and manifestation as a human. So just know that if somebody has emotional cords and dirt in their snow globe they will just "magically" imagine that it is there. And what we must say is many people will say, 'I must just be imagining this, I must just be making this up,' and what we must say is 'Why would you be making this up over anything else? Why would you be making it up?' The grand thing about this snow globe and the encryption that we're putting into this book is that there are no expectations of anything. Somebody isn't actually visualizing themselves. They're not actually visualizing their chakras. They're not actually visualizing layers of their body and aura. They are visualizing a snow globe with no attachment to what appears in their mind. Because of this they will accurately see what is in their field."

JOE: The first topic are the cords, the attachments and the spirit --?

JESUS: *"Well, first we must teach how to connect with the higher self, connect with the Christ light, so that --."*

JOE: After the snow globe has been established?

JESUS: "After it's visualized, yes. Once one has visualized and seen what the snow globe looks like, what they must do is take their attention to just above the solar plexus and below the heart. So... the bottom of the ribs, in between the ribs, this is where the spirit resides in the physical body. This is where your spirit burns bright. One can take their awareness or their focus to this area and see or sometimes feel this bubble of light within their statue. Some days this bubble of light may be very bright and big; some days it may be very dim and small. Some days it may almost be non-existent. What one must do is imagine that a big huge, bright light from above the snow globe is shooting in from the top of it, down into the bubble that is inside the statue --.

JOE: Like a laser beam?

JESUS: "Yes. A laser beam is one way to see it, some see a waterfall, this channel sees a beautiful bright crystalline mercury-like liquid... What many may see this as is another bright snow globe way up above them, dropping down to about six feet above their space. This upper snow globe representing the statue's higher self/creator soul will send energy, that could look like a laser beam, down into their snow globe, down into the statue, and into the seat of their soul or in other words the bubble between their ribs. All they must do is just watch as the white laser beam or light fills up their spirit bubble and begins to grow the bubble out, and as it's growing out it's pushing out all of the negative energy, all of the negative emotions, feelings, and experiences... all of the negativity that is within that person's snow globe and releasing it from their space. Sometimes it will take one minute, sometimes it will take somebody 20 minutes to watch as this laser beam of white energy fills up their bubble and pushes out until the light becomes the same size as their snow globe. Once this is done then they are done with a basic connecting with their creator, filling themselves with the light of their creator, and pushing out the energies that are not for their highest and best good.

Emotions are Contagious

These include energies that belong to other people. And when we say 'energy' we mean floating emotions. Energy is just simply emotions. And these emotions get stuck to people. If somebody has never dealt with anger, they do not have defense mechanisms for anger. So if they are at the grocery store and they get somebody's anger within their snow globe they may have an anxiety attack and wonder why they are having an anxiety attack. It's because something that the person next to them very easily deals with – because they have defense mechanisms, so it is not bothering them – but gets into their snow globe and now they are having a panic attack. Or they don't have a panic attack and they go home with this anger energy in their snow globe and they begin to take the anger out on their children or their wife, or their husband, or their coworkers. They begin to act out this anger. Because every human being, every human being is a product of the snowflakes that are around them."

JOE: Well then if I, Joe, visualize my snow globe and then I visualize my big-Joe, or my soul, six feet above me in another snow globe, and I see this beam of magnificent light come through the snow globe into my solar plexus, lighting up the Holy Spirit within me, which blows out all the negativity that has been attached to me, and then I go out into the world and go to work or I go see my girlfriend, or whoever it is I am with, it would seem to me that I'm protected from that negative energy.

JESUS: "Yes, absolutely you are."

JOE: But how does the negative energy reattach and how often should we be re-establishing the snow globe and the attachment to our soul?

The Guides Discuss Frequency

PETER AND MARY: "Once a day connecting with your soul is good enough. You do not have to go through a full process of watching the energy come in. If you forget to do this and you're driving to work, you can call in the energy of your creator into your snow globe and just say, 'Let's do this, help me today.' Because remember, you have to invite your guides, you have to invite your guardians in. You have to invite your masters in, in order for them to be able to help you. What many don't understand is that you may ask for protection and when you ask for protection – let's look at this in numbers: let us just say that source energy exists at 100,000 megahertz, let us just say." [This is Jesus now. It was Peter and Mary before. Now it's Jesus. He always comes in with the simple things.]

JESUS: "Let us just say that source energy, or the light of all creation that has created all of us, exists at 100,000 megahertz. This is the source of all creation and is emitting its light upon all of its creations. Then let us just say that a human being's physical body exists at, let's say, 100 megahertz. So this is a very dense frequency. Human emotions exist under 100, and they will get into your snow globe and they will make the physical body sick because they are bringing the frequency down even lower.

When one calls in the source energy into the snow globe, this 100,000 megahertz light that is being emitted from the center of all creation is coming down through your creator self (your Soul's snow globe)– and let's just say that your creator self has a 1,000 megahertz so that when it comes down into your field the light melts away all the low frequencies. So as with anything, if something is going very very fast next to something that is very very slow, the very very slow spinning thing is going to speed up so that it will start going the same speed as the fast thing. Or, the fast thing will slow down to meet the slow thing half way through. But the energy of your creator soul, 1,000 megahertz, is withstanding, it never changes, so it's always holding itself at 1,000...1,000...1,000. So when you call this into you it holds its energy up very high and pulls your frequency, or pulls your vibration up. Everybody always speaks of 'raise your vibration, raise your vibration, raise your vibration.' This is what this speaks of. It is the calling in of a higher vibration into your snow globe so that the lower things go away. Now, if you were to go with your girlfriend and your girlfriend has a frequency, let's say, of 25, because there is anger. Perhaps she has cords attached to other snow globes that belong to other people like say her daughter who has a frequency level of 11. She then will have a snow globe that has a spiritual credit score of 11 even though she is at 25. This 11 is like a trade line weighing her down. So now she is a lower frequency and because the two of you are connecting with a cord between your snow globes, you can sometimes get some of her energy if your energy is not protected. As long as your frequency is higher than hers you will not take on any of her energy. But let us just say that she says something to provoke you or make you mad, or somebody cuts you off on the freeway, or somebody does something to make you very upset, and you drop below her frequency, then all of her stuff will start coming into your snow globe even though you had asked for protection. It's because you are now down in the lower astral plane. We speak of the spiritual credit score much in this channel's classes and we have channeled much information for a book that will be called 'What is Your Spiritual Credit Score' and we do not want to include this in this book but what we would like to include in this is different levels of consciousness, say 1 through 10. So if you are at 5, your girlfriend is at 3, she may pull you down to 4. But if you are calling in and connecting in with your creator self, you will be able to stay at 5; she is at 3. So most likely you will end up healing her and bringing her up to 5. So a lot of her stuff will get healed just by you being around her. And this is why we love this book so much, because what we are going to be doing is we are going to be teaching people to raise their vibrations using their creator self – not the Creator, not God, we can say the Christ light if you would like, but it is the Creator that created the soul that is in us. This is a high enough frequency to sustain a much higher conscious level of human beings. So if even five percent of the planet began to fill their snow globe with the light of their creator self, they would begin healing all of their family members that were not doing this. They would begin healing their coworkers that were not doing this because their frequency is higher, and just the mere fact that they are next to somebody, they are going to be raising that person's vibration. That is why this book is so beautiful, indeed. And this is the book that we have been speaking of that will be a best seller."

JOE: If I, Joe, set up my snow globe, I've cleaned it out and now it's crystal clear and I've got nice, white flakes floating down, no more black flakes, or no crud on the bottom of the snow globe, and I am clean as a whistle, but now I'm heading out to work and I've got a boss and I've got coworkers who are just nasty individuals and every time I walk in the front door to go to work I just feel like I've got crud all over me and I immediately turn into a bad mood. How can I overcome that short of quitting my job and going and finding another?   Which, maybe that's what you are telling me to do, but how do I retain that light, how do I retain that exalted energy that I've used to clean out my snow globe when I'm around all this crud that is just driving me nuts?

MARISA: Peter says, "Let's all quit our jobs!" and he put a Tommy Bahama shirt on and he just threw a hammock over his shoulder and said, "Let's all quit our jobs!"

JOE: That's not the right answer. You've still got to pay your rent, you still have to buy food, you still have to pay for the car, you've still got to pay for the babysitter and you still have to pay for this, and pay for that.

MARISA: Peter's like, "Alright, alright!" That is so funny. Jesus is huge today. And Rosemary is here. Rosemary is like, "Look at my snow globe, I'm a carousel." And she has a little carousel on the inside. It's playing music and she's like dancing around in circles. (*Rosemary is a central figure in our Conversations books from The Bible Speaks series. Basically she was a close friend of Mary, the sister of Lazarus but also quite a Jesus groupie. She acts and talks like a "valley girl"*).

JOE: So when your snow globe walks into this darkness, darkness of your job, how do you retain that light, how do you retain that beautiful energy that you had before you walked into that mess? And this ties into relationships as well….jobs and relationships.

JESUS: "Well, let us just say this. If somebody is not affected emotionally, their energy will not be open for other's energy to get into them. So this is why many people that are emotionally shut down are not affected by other peoples' energy around them. You can look at them and there can be chaos and it won't even phase them because they are emotionally shut down. People do this for many reasons. Either they were very sensitive as a child so they shut down because it was not comfortable, or their soul chose that they were not going to be a sensitive individual. Let us rewind very quick so we can bring an understanding to the different frequencies of human beings and also just bring a very quick understanding to those who want to understand what someone like you, Joe, as an empathic person, you can feel other people's emotions. For we have talked in the past books about the two 12 story buildings. We have the one building that has a 3 on it and represents the third dimension (physical) and one 12 story building right next to it that has a 4 on it and represents the fourth dimension or astral plane. If our consciousness or our awareness, stays grounded within building 3, we cannot feel anything that is in building 4 which is the spirit world, the dream world, emotions, feelings, memories, etc..."

JOE: Wait a minute. I thought that we are one building and there were lower, not separate buildings. I picture myself as a 12-story building with all these floors. I've got 12 floors. But inside each floor are lots of rooms which are different parts of my existence and my experiences. So we've got to keep it simple here.

MARISA: It's simple.

JOE: People who have never read anything that we've ever written are going to go, 'What are they talking about?'

How to rise above the muck

JESUS: Okay, so let's keep it very simple. "If you are inside your statue..." [So scratch all that about the buildings.] "If you are inside your statue, you will not feel other people's emotions. You will not feel other people's feelings because you are inside your statue, inside your energy. As the vibration of the planet goes up -- we speak of how the planet is shifting. Anyone who is reading this may have heard the vibration of the planet is going up after 2012..."

JOE: Wait, stop, stop.   You've gone off on a tangent. I asked a very specific question. I said, I've got the snow globe, I've set up my snow globe, I have received that laser light, I have cleaned out my snow globe. I am pure, I feel good, I feel like I can take on the world, and then I get in my car and I'm getting closer and closer to work, and I can feel that negativity starting to come into my snow globe and then I walk into work and that creepy boss that drives me nuts is right there giving me that dirty look and then my suitemate next to me is screaming out loud about her kids and her terrible life, and all I want to do is get my work done and I can just feel the darkness sneaking back into me. How do I overcome that, short of quitting my job? How do I keep my snow globe clean without thinking about floors of buildings and thinking about the universal energy and this, that, and the other? How do I keep it simple? How do I keep my snow globe clean when I'm surrounded by muck that I know I have to endure because I've got to pay the babysitter, I've got to pay for my car, I've got to pay for my house --?

JESUS: *"This was why we are speaking of the upper and lower levels, because there is the lower astral plane, the upper astral plane. When you are walking into a building, if your vibration is high, no matter how angry people are no matter how grumpy people are, no matter how extremely irritated people are, if somebody is above the lower astral plane, they will not feel it. This is why we speak of, if your consciousness is within your statue, within your field, and your vibration is high, you won't feel it. Instead of getting irritated, instead of getting sad, instead of getting mad at the people around you, you will say, 'Oh, I feel bad for them, they are dealing with a lot, oh well, better go about my work'."*

JOE: That's the energy of being --.

JESUS: *Compassionate.*

JOE: --protected by the snow globe?

JESUS: *"Yes, this is the energy of being compassionate towards others. Instead of getting wrapped up and entangled within their emotions, you are feeling compassion for them, but you are not*

45

entangling with them. And this is why people need to understand that you can entangle with others if you are emotionally feeling for them, or if you are looking at them and they are screaming at their wife, or their wife is screaming at them, [and you're] thinking, 'Oh I remember the last time that happened to me...' and now your snow globes are connected, and now you're taking on all their gunk, if you are empathic.

Everyone is an Empath

So what we were trying to explain was that, as the vibration of the planet has shifted, there used to be the case where some people were empathic and some people were not. Some people could feel other peoples' emotions, and some people could not. Now, everyone can feel everyone's emotions because we have shifted to a different frequency on this planet. We have shifted into a different dimension. So, prior to 2012 you may not have had so many sympathy pains when you watched a movie, you may not have felt the pain of watching somebody get hurt on TV. But now after 2012, you do, and it will continue to get worse and worse, and worse. Or shall we say 'better and better and better'? Because the more people that can feel the other people around them, the more people are going to care about the other people around them. If somebody is going to go and hurt people, or rob a building, or do something to hurt a woman, and they feel the pain the woman is feeling, or the hurt the woman is feeling, they are not going to do it because they can feel how horrible it is. They are not going to get any satisfaction out of it. So when we say it's going to get worse and worse, what we mean is, yes, it will get worse and worse for people until they realize, 'I'm feeling other people's emotions around me, I'm feeling the person's emotions on TV that I'm watching, this horror movie,

I'm experiencing it, because it's in my snow globe now...' because there's really no glass anymore, everyone's snowflakes are combining, and this is why there is so much more cancer, there is so much more brain aneurysms, ulcers, people are dying of cancers, they are dying of lung cancer from never smoking. It's because people's physical bodies are now being affected by all the emotions around them that they never felt before, but now they do. So when you walk into your office, one extra precautionary thing that one can do is you can imagine going up one floor, just imagine you are going up above all of the muck with your snow globe filled with light, and then go to work. This will – without going into lower, upper, middle astral planes, or different levels of the astral plane – this will give people a simple visualization. They can imagine that they are on an elevator, they can imagine they are in their snow globe and they can go up to the safest possible floor for them to be on, and then go into the office. And we guarantee that they will not be as upset, they will not be as irritated by the people around them. This is just how it works. If you are in the muck with them, whether it's their muck or your own muck, you are going to get irritated. The man griping next to you is going to irritate you. The boss that is rude is going to irritate you. If you are up higher, you're going to look at the boss and say, 'I'm so happy I'm not him, poor guy, was probably abused as a child, oh wow, it must be miserable being him; you know, I'm just going to send him some light instead of taking his mood personally, instead of thinking that he's out to get me. Because when you're at the lower frequencies, if you're at the lower "spiritual credit scores", everything is an attack, everything – people are against you, you, you, me, me, me, I, I, I. But as we get into an "I Am" consciousness where we are all one, we feel compassion for others that are not happy. Does this make sense?"

JOE: It makes sense. I can picture that as I'm walking up to the front door of my job and I know I'm going to walk into all this darkness, before I open that door, I'm going to visualize my snow globe getting on the elevator and rising up above the darkness, and that's where I will be. Where the light is. And then I can walk into the door at the new level, at the second level. Yes, and my compassion will hopefully help to raise the energy of those below me by them seeing my light.

JESUS: "Yes, and this is the beauty of it. Many people will just look at you, even now, Joe, and say 'Wow, you just look like a happy guy.' They don't understand what it is. They just know that you feel happy. You look at people like Mother Theresa. You look at people like the Pope or the Dalai Lama. You look at the people that just seem to emanate light. These people, yes, they are in a physical body, but their consciousness – they are up several floors above everybody, up above the muck, but they are still emitting so much of their light down through the muck and helping to clean it and cleanse it and clear it."

JOE: For those that are in rough relationships, a man loves his wife, the wife loves the husband, but each has irritating qualities that doesn't bring out the full happiness that they should have. They don't want to split up, they don't want to get a divorce. Maybe they even have children. But maybe each of them are starting to feel trapped in this negativity every time they have to go home. Is this the same example you'd use as your job? Do you visualize yourself rising up above to the ceiling, to the roof of the house, as you enter the house, in your light, so that you're above the fray? But if you're above the fray and your wife starts barking at you the minute you walk in, and the baby starts crying uncontrollably and all of a sudden you just know that that's the time when you get so irritated then if you've visualized yourself going up that extra floor and being a bright clear snow globe, is that going to help? Will it help?

JESUS: "Yes, that will help, but what we would like to say is, the very first advice we give in any relationship issues, the very first advice that we give to those that pray to us, those who ask advice of us, is that, in most relationships those things that the couples are accusing each other of are their own snowflakes. So let us just put it like this. Joe, your very first wife, she had within her snow globe cheating energy. She was cheating. So she had cheating energy, let us just say this is green energy, these are dark green snowflakes, jealous cheating energy swirling around in her snow globe. If she was home alone or if she was out with friends doing whatever she was doing but not paying attention to her emotional body – (because the emotions are the snowflakes and when you're in your statue you are not feeling your emotions) – not paying attention to her snowflakes, but then you get home, her emotional body, because she loves you or feels something for you, is invoked, so she begins to feel her snowflakes, she looks at you and she says, 'You're cheating!' when in reality she is seeing her own snowflakes first."

JOE: She is looking through her own snow globe.

JESUS: "She is looking through her own snow globe. So people always see their own flakes first, their own flakes first" --.

JOE: And they project those flakes onto the other person? In *Heaven Speaks* we pointed that out as one pointing a finger at themselves in a mirror when accusing someone else for something that they themselves are actually guilty of.

JESUS: "*The other person. So this example of this channel, before she understood this idea of projection and seeing her own snowflakes first, she thought she was so intuitive, she always thought she always knew how people were feeling, she always would feel what they were feeling, but what she did not realize is that she was feeling her own snowflakes, but she had no idea of what her snowflakes were because she didn't know herself. So when she would get home she would say, 'You're in a bad mood, you're having a horrible day, you're in a bad mood...' and her husband would say, 'No, I'm not but I'm going to get in a bad mood if you keep telling me I'm in a bad mood...' and then they would start fighting. What she didn't understand was she was an empath, so she may have passed by somebody at the office, she may have passed by somebody at the grocery store that was in a bad mood, and it got into her snow globe. So the first emotional person she was with would be her husband and....*"

JOE: ...now, wait for a second. You keep referring to everybody being in their snow globes. My understanding is we're void of snow globes unless we ask to be protected by the snow globe.

JESUS: "*No, we are all a snow globe.*"

JOE: Everybody is a snow globe?

JESUS: "We are a snow globe. Our physical body --. Oh, let's make this very clear. The snow globe is a representation of our entire energy field. The statue in the middle is our physical body, the snowflakes are our emotions, our feelings, our memories, all of these things that we have ever experienced our entire life. So let us get into the part where – we will get back to relationships – but let us just explain what happens and how one goes to live in a snow globe. We will make this very simple. You are a spirit, Joe, you are living in heaven. You say, 'I am going to go down to earth and I'm going to be born to Joe and Betty Moris, I'm going to be their child.' So you go and you research them, you study them, you spend time in their snow globes, you as a soul go into their snow globes and you hang around them, you look to see what their energy feels like, you look to see how they react to each other, you look to see where they live...Its kind of like going into a movie theater when you go into someone else's snow globe, it's like going into their movie. You look to see what it's like, you tell your guide, you say, 'Okay, Adam, okay Jesus, I think I want to be one of their kids, I've lived with them before but not in those snow globes, I've lived with them as other human beings, but I'm ready to be their child.' So they conceive you, you go, you are born, and from the second you are born into a physical body you now have a statue, your spirit lives inside the statue, and around you is *a ball, and this is a glass ball with water and swirling energy inside of it like a snow globe, and all of your snowflakes are pure white, pure white. You are completely crystal clean, completely clear. There are guides, there are angels that protect your snow globe so that no one else's snowflakes will get into your snow globe. For the first three years, no one else's snowflakes can get into your snow globe. Because this would affect your life path. This would affect your planning that your higher self and Christ planned for your spirit. But we will not get too deeply into that right now (*mostly covered in Heaven Speaks*). At about age three, this is when the human mind begins to develop itself and free will begins. When free will begins, this is when one can pick up other peoples' energies. This is usually when one will cut off their direct connection from Source down into their spirit inside their snow globe. This connection will get cut, or a knot will be tied in it, or something will decrease the connection with Source, and that's the mind. The mind starts saying, 'Hmm, no, this is a physical reality, I'm not a spirit, I'm a human being.' So this cuts off a majority of the energy coming in from the higher self or creator soul. Because the snow globe still needs energy the child starts drawing in energy from their parent's snow globes rather than the high self. So let us just say, you are three years old, Mom is jealous so she's got green energy, Dad is angry, so he's got red energy.*

So now, instead of being pure white, you now have white, red, and green snowflakes swirling around in your snow globe. It doesn't feel very good so this is when children begin to act up, they start acting either angry or jealous (depending on the characteristics of the energy they are not surrounded with from parents, siblings, teachers, friends, etc....) They don't know how to handle these adult emotions that are in their snow globe. So they start to act up. Or they build up very strong defense mechanisms. They might block their emotions so that they cannot feel these things. Either way, they don't clear their energy because they don't know how so it just stays there. After they become use to it, defenses are built up, it doesn't affect them much until they get older and get into, say, their first relationship. So you are now older and still carrying around all those red and green snowflakes in your snow globe and you haven't learned how to clean them out. You begin your first relationship and you've got jealous energy and angry energy floating around in your field, but your brain has blocked these, and you're the happiest guy, the most un-jealous guy in the world because your defense mechanisms have said 'I'm not going to be angry, and I'm not going to be jealous, so I'm going to be exactly opposite, because that's what my defense mechanisms are telling me to do...' So you get into a relationship with a girl, and everything is fine, you like her statue, she likes yours. She thinks *your statue is good looking, your mind is amazing, your ego, you look great. You think the same about her. The two of you like each other. You go out. You kiss for the first time but then two weeks into the relationship (*it could be two weeks or two months...this is just an example*) the emotional bodies open and what happens is you get a cord between the two of you. Now you have a cord attached to each other and then here comes all of your green and red snowflakes into her field. Now all of a sudden she's telling her friends, 'he was the nicest guy, oh my gosh, but now he's so jealous and angry, everything he does is jealous and angry...' When really you're not. She's just feeling your snowflakes. And then let's say that maybe she had a depressed father and she has dark blue snowflakes in her snow globe so all of a sudden now you're telling your buddies, 'Man, she was so cool but now I get so depressed around her, she's just so depressing...' And that's when couples break up. They just don't give each other the time of day because what has happened is, they're feeling each other's snowflakes now instead of each other's statues. So if more people can understand this on this planet, they will begin to see, 'my goodness, if I clear my snow globe before I start dating somebody, and I clear out all my snowflakes, they'll always get to see me as me, not me as my parents, or me as my ex, or me as my friends'. Because of the energies of this planet* *everyone has become so sensitive that it is almost impossible to cut through and not feel the emotions that somebody has in their snow globe, whether they are that person's or not. So when a couple is together, what they must truly see and what they must understand is that they must clear their energy. And if they clear their energy, then it is less likely they will be blaming each other for things that not only they would be doing, but things that are in their field. So let us just say that two girls, two girls are married. One is getting a divorce, the other one is happily married. Friend A is happily married; Friend B is getting a divorce. Friend B's husband is cheating on her and she is leaving him, and he hates her and she hates him. Friend A is hanging out with Friend B a lot, so they are merging energies. Friend A, if she is not careful, will begin to think that her husband hates her because she is taking on Friend B's energy that says 'my husband hates me.' So if she is not careful she will start perceiving that her husband hates her. So if Friend A's husband doesn't open the door for her, usually she would be just like, 'Oh he didn't open the door for me,' but now it's like, 'He hates me, he didn't open the door for me.' So now, she begins picking fights with him and now they start arguing."*

JOE: Back to the point, not to interrupt, but at that point when she is feeling those emotions, what does she do? Does she reconnect with --?

JESUS: *"Yes."*

JOE:　　--the snow globe that's six feet above and say, "Please, please, clean me out..."

JESUS: *"Yes."*

JOE:　　-- "Just get this darkness off of me, get this doubt away from me" ...?

JESUS: *"Yes, this is when you call in the energy from the soul's energy, call it back into the snow globe, reconnect and push out any energy that does not belong to you."*

JOE:　　And this is a form of praying?

JESUS: *"Yes."*

JOE:　　Or a form of meditation?

JESUS: *"Yes."*

JOE:　　And it can only take moments? In the blink of an eye you can achieve this?

JESUS: *"Yes, yes, absolutely."*

JOE:　　This is simple. This isn't something where somebody has to be like a Muslim and get down on their prayer rugs and pray five times a day, you know, praying to Allah saying "Oh please, please Allah, blah, blah, blah." Or "Jesus, I feel so guilty, I should be reading the Bible right now so that you'll protect me." They can do this in the blink of an eye, in their faith, that that snow globe of their soul is always with them?

JESUS: "Yes."

JOE: But because of our free will, our soul's snow globe will not act on its own?

JESUS: "Exactly, exactly."

JOE: So we have to use our free will to get back to our upper snow globe to bring us back that laser energy to clean us out?

JESUS: "Absolutely, and truly, truly, people can clear themselves 50 times a day if they would like to. But the absolute key here is human beings becoming more conscious. As human beings become more conscious, they become more aware of their emotions as they're passing through, and they say, 'I don't think that's my emotion, okay, release that, push that out.' So you can use that and tell that emotion to go away. Because many times emotions will begin piling up in someone's snow globe and they won't notice until they have blown up and screamed at everybody in the house, and told everyone to go away, or ran off on their own, or broken up with their boyfriend or their girlfriend, or blamed it on the kids, or done something to where now they have to turn around and say sorry with their tail between their legs and go back, when really what they were doing was they were reacting to the man that sits next to them in the cubicle's energy of the nagging wife. For this channel has had an occurrence where her husband would come home and whenever he would come home after working with a certain person, they would get in a fight. It is because that person had a wife that nagged him constantly. So when her husband would come home, she would think that he was calling her a nag. She thought he was calling her a nag even though he would never call her a nag. They came to the conclusion that every time he worked with this individual they would get in a fight. So now when he works with him, he says, 'I worked with this person today,' and they both clear their energy together and then they don't get in a fight."

JOE: You know what? We have covered every one of the topics that we were supposed to cover for today except for the wrap up, and that was the manifestation. Does Jesus want to touch on the manifestation?

MARISA: Yeah.

JOE: Okay, to wrap this all up, it's a short book,

it's a short taping, and I think we can put this all together. The last thing was manifestation. But I think we covered the manifestation. We manifest our life by how we want to keep our snow globe clean and where we want to place our snow globe. If we want to immerse our snow globe into the muck and the mess and everything else that's around us, then we are consciously allowing ourselves to bring in the darker snowflakes and all the emotions of the world around us. But, we can manifest a much cleaner life that allows us to pursue the plan that is within our statue, which is our spirit, which has been set before we were born, by envisioning ourselves rising up with the energy, being above the darkness, and allowing the darkness to see the light above them, which is ourselves, and I guess in our own faith we will manifest the life that our creator has planned for us to follow.

JESUS: "Yes..."

JOE: Is that the manifestation that Jesus talks about?

JESUS: "Well, yes, yes. But following one's path is very important and by not only calling in this laser beam light from the creator self into your statue, not only are you calling in light but also high frequency energy to blast out low frequency energy; the low frequency muck that can cause you to perceive life in a way that life really isn't. If one is perceiving life through jealous eyes, or through defensive eyes, they are always going to think people are attacking them. So their day will be very different from if they were to clear out their snow globe. When we speak of manifestation, yes, by following the soul's energy, the soul's frequency, the consciousness, or the information from the soul, is also being downloaded into the snow globe, so this isn't something that we got into, but it's also allowing people to begin to remember what their path is, their intuition will get stronger, their faith will get stronger in their life and in their path, and where they are going and what they need to do. They will just know things. So, this is something that, in addition to feeling better, will also bring a closer connection to God and a knowing of what you are here to do. When we speak of manifestation, what we speak of is an exercise that people can do. They can wake up each morning and they can make a list of things that they need to get completed. We will not get into the specifics of how energy works and how beliefs work and how cords work and things like this but we will discuss cords in this book a little bit more in depth because we spoke of it, about people being connected, but we do not speak of how people bring the same type of person back into their life if they have a – well, we will just touch on this really quick and then go into manifestation and then be done. If you, say, have a cord connected to that first wife with the green, jealous, cheating energy, what will happen, Joe, is she will be gone, her statue will have moved on. But, if you have a cord connected to a snow globe with green, jealous energy, the way the universe works, the way the energy works, and we will not go into depth of how it works, but we will just say that you will always pull somebody in with green energy. You will continue to pull people into your life that have green energy. The other option would be that you will pull someone in that doesn't have any green energy, but as soon as you begin to open up to them emotionally, you will think they have green energy, you will think they're going to leave you, you will think they're going to cheat on you, you will think that they're jealous because you are still corded up to this green energy that is feeding into your snow globe, so you're reading this."

JOE: Does that mean then that I, through that same cord, am sending those same green and red snowflakes through to that person that I've now fallen in love with?   And that person will then manifest that life I expected her to do, and end up becoming an angry and cheating person, when they never even thought of being a cheater?

JESUS: "Sometimes it can happen like this if one is, let us just say...."

JOE: In other words, if my energy has forced them to become what I was afraid they were going to become.

JESUS: *"Yes. Exactly."*

JOE: So how do I cut that cord? How do I make sure that isn't going to happen?

JESUS: *"All you must do is, when you connect with the higher self, you must communicate with your higher self that there is a specific thing that you are cutting. You can't just say 'cut all my cords' because that will work for about one minute. All of your cords will be cut yes but it isn't specific enough instruction to your Source, your Soul, your higher self (don't forget that your soul, your higher self will not override your free will). You have to say and you have to determine who it's to, or what it's about. Say I'm feeling very jealous, and when you are calling in this energy from your soul into your spirit that's expanding out, while it's expanding out, say, 'Cut any cords that are attached to jealousy, cut any cords that are attached to relationships where people cheated on me.' You don't have to be very ritualistic about this. Just have a conversation with the spirit world above you and say, 'I need all the cords cut that are connected to someone who cheated on me,' or 'somebody who was jealous.' 'Please cut all these cords.' And then you can actually, if you are very imaginative, you will actually be able to feel or sense where the cord was, and you will actually visualize seeing a cord on the outside of your snow globe being cut. If not...."*

JOE: Is this something I have to do every day?

JESUS: "No, this is just when things start to come up. Let's say that you are in your relationship now with your girlfriend, and you begin to fear that she's going to leave you or you're going to fear that she's with somebody else, you can call in this laser beam energy and ask that any cords that you have that may have gone back to past relationships which brought on a lot of jealous energy because of say, your mother, this energy was in your field which may have manifested the relationships that you manifested because of the situation between your parents – one going out on the other. So this energy was in your field. So this may have attracted that type of person to you. So the way the energy works is it goes back and forth between the people. There is nobody at fault, nobody to blame. Energy is just energy. And this is the whole reason, the whole reason behind a spirit wanting an earthly human experience. It's just fun because we don't know what's going to affect us. But now that the vibration of the planet has gone up we have more control over these energies and this is what we were going in to teach people in the Bible days, in the days of my ministry.

These were the teachings of Christ

*We were teaching people how to fill themselves with the Holy Spirit (*creator soul/higher self), *fill themselves with the Holy Spirit which would push out and dissolve the negative human emotions* (forgiveness), *which would push out the pain, and would cause them to have more compassion for each other. 'Do unto others what you would have them do unto you.' This, the snow globe is the whole basis of my teachings."*

JOE: Wow! That makes sense!!

JESUS: "This is my teachings. The snow globe is the basis of my teachings. If everybody could just understand this simply, not everybody's problems are going to go away, they are still going to have their own energy, they are still going to have their own issues, their own beliefs, their own things they need to work on, but people have enough issues on their own within themselves, they don't need other people's issues on them, too. So Joe, if you are starting to feel insecure, [about] your girlfriend, you feel as if she is being distant, or you feel as if she's thinking of somebody else or wanting to leave, this may be energy from an old relationship that you may still be corded to. Sometimes you can cut a cord and it will be gone forever. Other times you may have hundreds of cords to that person and let us just say one of the cords is to (my last ex) *leaving, one of the cords is to her meeting somebody else, one of them is to her being controlling, one of them is to her looking down on you, one of them is to her not respecting you or not believing in you, and not relying on you, and trusting you, so you have all these different things that are kind of corded to this one person but they are separate traits (and different colored snowflakes). So when you start to get upset inside, before getting upset outwardly or getting insecure, you can stop, connect with your snow globe, and ask that any energies that are causing you to feel this way be cut and removed. And once the snow globe, once your energy, your light energy within you has expanded out to the size of your snow globe, you know it's done. And really, truly, and we don't need to put this in the book because we don't want people that are not Christian and not into Jesus and all of us..." [Peter is like "Yeah!"] "But what it is, is it's me coming in and I'm doing this for you. I'm the one who is clearing, I'm cleaning, I'm cleansing, and also so are all your guides. So really all of us are the ones that are in here. So the only job you have is the visualizing of the light expanding and just knowing that it will be done and we handle the rest."*

JOE: When you say "It is I, Jesus, doing this" is

that through your surrogate, the soul? I mean if there are one million people all talking to you at the same time saying, "Clean out my snow globe, clean out my snow globe," are they really talking to you, or are they talking to your creation, which is each person's soul?

JESUS: *"Yes, you are talking to the creator of that which I am, which is Christ. This is the ninth layer of us, the Christ light, that comes in and does all of this, but understand when you connect with your soul all of your guides are alerted and I am your personal master guide (every human has a Master guide, Jesus is not everyone's guide there are 1000's of Masters that are here helping the human souls they are assigned to), so I specifically will help you. So if you don't know what's wrong, if you say, 'I don't know who this cord is connected to, I don't know what's going on,' maybe you got off the phone with a client who is going through financial issues and now all of a sudden you're so worried about money, but this person didn't talk to you about worrying about money, now you're worrying about money, now you're wondering if you should ever be in this relationship with this person, and do they need you to take care of them, and you start worrying about things that you would never worry about. You can just connect in with your snow globe and as its expanding out just say, 'Cut any cords to anything that's causing this worry, cut any cords to anything that's causing this drama within my mind,' and you will feel a release, you will feel a release. You don't need to know what was connected, is our point. You don't need to know what it was connected to."*

JOE: I'm picturing my guide, my angels with brooms in their hands sweeping these dirty snowflakes out of my snow globe.

PETER: "And this is what we are doing."

MARISA: [That's what Peter just said.]

PETER: "And this is what we are doing. We are getting rid of those. We are cleaning house, we are cleaning house, because it is time to clean the house of the earth plane because the earth plane is dirty. Emotions everywhere, no one knows who they belong to, everybody is blaming everybody for everything else. Look at your relationship, look how shut down your girlfriend was until she saw that you were good with a child. This child changed your relationship because prior to this she was with men who left, she was with men who did not like children, who did not want to be responsible with children, so she still saw you as them because she was corded to them. When this channel (Marisa) did the healing on your girlfriend six months ago and cut all the cords, your girlfriend began to see you for you, even though she still had a belief that men leave when kids are coming into her life. When she saw you were good with her grandchild, the cord cut itself. It dismissed itself because that belief system that she had was now eradicated from her field. So sometimes cords will heal themselves, other times the pesky cords will keep bringing the same thing back into your life, but then you have to ask yourself, was she really with men that didn't like kids, or did she just think it, so she left before the kids came into the picture? It started because the first man she was with and corded to didn't want a kid. Because this is what was happening, when she had to start raising her abandoned grandchild, she and you split up because of the way she pushed you away, because in her mind she was reading the cord that she had to the person she was with that didn't want to be with her with a child. Does this make sense?"

JOE: This makes sense. Things really changed once she saw how much I cared for her grandchild who we are now attempting to adopt together. Okay, I think that kind of wraps up the manifestation, I hope.

JESUS: No, the manifestation --. "What we would like is, we want to give everybody something really fun to do with their snow globe. Everybody thinks emotions are great and feeling good --."

JOE: Is this the epilogue, is this the ending?

JESUS: Yes, this is the end. This is an exercise that we can put in the beginning.

JOE: And who is this coming from? Is this Peter or Jesus?

MARISA: This is Jesus and Peter together. They're kind of like going back and forth like they're singing a song.

JOE: So this is the epilogue to the book, the snow globe book?

A note from Marisa

The snow globe is meant to be an intuitive exercise for those who are or are not intuitive and it is also meant to be a tool for intuitive adults and children to take their skills and abilities to a new, quantum level of understanding.

The Snow Globe has been the most proven tool in teaching beginners and advanced students to learn to read energy by not just sporadically seeing or feeling it's presence but to call it in, see it, and understand it enough to relay messages to others or self about the nature of the aura and energetic structure in question.

The amazing thing about the Snow Globe is it can be as simple or as complex as you would like it to be while the results stay equally effective no matter which route you choose to take. The reason is because it is not you healing you... it is you calling upon a higher aspect of you to clear you while you witness or imagine it being done! It's brilliant because it takes complex quantum energy healing concepts and makes it so that ANYone can do it! I thank my guide for the gift of the snow globe every day!

Once you have the simple structure of connecting to and embodying your higher self by imagining that you are inside the lit up area just below the heart and allowing a beam of light coming from a snow globe above you to fill up and expand the lit up area through your entire snow globe you may feel pulled to visualize something that is not in these steps. That is GREAT! That is your Higher Self communicating with you! Good Job!!

MY ONLY WARNING IS and THIS IS VERY IMPORTANT .... Do NOT imagine pulling energy from anywhere other than DIRECTLY above you. Directly above you is all the layers of source, your soul, and the Christ light. To the sides of you and in front of you (and this is not meant to scare you rather it is to empower you in knowing you CONTROL what is in your snow globe and it is universal low that if you tell something to leave it MUST leave!) are other beings that will pose as source to unsuspecting newbies and even long time mediums, healers, and channels who cannot see the way I can see or have just not dug around and asked the same questions I have harassed the other side with when it comes to the structure of reality and all the things that clairvoyants see. I am SUPER nosey!! (hehe) It took me a few years to chart out where all beings stand and now teach a class on this chart. But for simplicity sake.... Only pull from above if you feel drawn to change the exercise. If you are interested in studying the Anatomy of the Soul or learning all about Angels, Guides, and Teachers, information can be found on my web site as well as free videos.

Step by Step Snow Globe Exercise
(Marisa's daily and nightly routine)

1)   Find a place where you can concentrate for 5 minutes
2)   Close your eyes
3)   Breathe in through your nose and out through your mouth a few times.

If it helps imagine a ball of light in front of your face with mist coming off of it. This is a ball of energy that will clean out your "distractions" and blockages keeping you from being able to concentrate. Imagine as you breathe in that you breathe in the mist and when you breathe out, breathe out the yucky stuff you have in your body or your mind like stress, anger, frustration... this can be your own feelings or "snow flakes" that you have taken on from others around you.

4)   Now that you feel somewhat settled, say in your head "Where am I right now?" Your awareness will most likely shift to somewhere other than in your head. It could be right outside your head or it could be 1000 miles away day dreaming about vacation or you could be at the office thinking of all you need to get done. In your mind say something like "Come back now, thank you" and imagine a little version of you moving in toward your mind. Keep in mind that you could very well be in one place or 500 so you may see that you are in lots of places. With your

imagination move the little you (consciousness) into the center of your brain. Once you can imagine that YOU are in the middle of your brain continue to breathe and feel what it feels like to be in your brain. Is it calm, busy, noisy, quiet, hot, cold, full, empty, etc…?

For more advanced students What does the little you look like right now? Does it look like you? Does it look like someone else? Is it a ball of light or an actual person? What color is the you that you are imagining? (This is NOT necessary to do but if you are an advanced student you can get a vast amount of information from how you see your consciousness at any given time. I write more about this in my snow globe exercise book on spiritual and intuition development.

5)   Next imagine that there is a ball 2 feet above your head. What color do you imagine it is? Make sure it is DIRECTLY ABOVE you and then with your mind imagine it dropping from STRAIGT above your head into your head. When it is surrounding the consciousness you just pulled into the middle of your brain imagine now that you are in that bubble, inside your brain and continue to breathe.

6) You may take a moment to feel what your mind feels like now. Has it slowed down or sped up? Is the texture and temperature the same? There is no correct or incorrect answer and this changes 1000's of times a day so don't judge yourself or get

frustrated over this step.

7) Now say "I am now a snow globe"

8) Imagine that you are a statue in the middle of the snow globe

9) Feel what the statue feels or imagine what the statue looks like

10) Imagine what it looks like from all directions (you can pretend there is a dressing room mirror in front and behind you so that you can see all sides of your statue....) is it a certain color, shape, or texture?

11) Now bring your awareness out to the water around the statue. What does it feel like? Does it have a goopy texture or is the water thin? If you were swimming in the water and looking through goggles would it appear Clear or Murky? What would it look like?

12) Imagine or think "if there were snowflakes in here what color would they be? What would they look like? Spend a moment experiencing and imagining what your snow globe feels and looks like.

13) Bring your awareness to the outside of your snow globe. Is the glass globe small or is your snow globe very large? Feel to see what this feels like.... imagine what it looks like. Is the glass cracked or dirty or is it clean and intact? Feel and imagine what it looks

and feels like from the inside and the outside. Let your imagination run wild!

NOW YOU HAVE CONNECTED WITH HIGHER SELF AND TUNED INTO YOUR ENERGY! GOOD JOB!

14) Drop the bubble in your mind down to the area just below your heart or imagine that a ball of energy drops from your head to this area below the heart and above the solar plexus in your "statue". This is the seat of your soul and is always shining bright even when you are covered in muck and can hardly see or feel it.

15) Imagine that you look up now to see a HUGE BRIGHT SHINING snow globe dropping down above you and stopping about 6 feet above you. Coming from it there is a LASER beam of energy, or liquid light dropping down into your snow globe, through your head, and pouring down into the seat of your soul just above the solar plexus.

16) As this energy pours into the bubble that your awareness is now in it begins to expand. It gets bigger and bigger transmuting ALL DARKNESS, all attachments, anything that is not YOU. As the bubble is infused with the energy from the higher snow globe the water becomes crystal clear, the snowflakes turn white, and any cracks or distortions to your glass are INSTANTLY repaired.

17) Once the seat of the soul is expanded out to the size of your snow globe you are done clearing yourself.

PROTECTION

18) Say "Shield my snow globe"

19) A beautiful golden liquid will pour down over your snow globe and coat it. You may imagine a a thick coat of paint pouring down over your snow globe until it is surrounding your entire snow globe. As you imagine the coating from above drying you can feel what it feels like to be cleansed clear protected and embodying your higher self.

20) Congratulations you Just did the Snow globe!

21) Keep on practicing!! You will grow to LOVE it just like we did!! You will begin to learn what certain colors feel like and what causes them. You will start to see when you are attached to other snow globes and when you are being drained by another person's snow globe.

22) Always do this exercise without agenda and without judgement. This is the glorious thing about the snow globe you are not looking at your energy or your chakras and you are not looking at YOU... You are looking at and feeling a snow globe so your mind releases attachment to judgement and makes it a fun and super effective multidimensional healing tool that ANYONE can do it. IF my dad is keeping his

energy clear using the snow globe ANYONE can!!

23) HAVE FUN!!

24) Move onto the Manifestation Exercise if desired!

Exercise to Manifest with your Snow Globe!

JESUS: "*This is an exercise in which we would like you to either put in the beginning of the book or the end of the book. We can mention it in the beginning of the book and say 'At the end of the book is an amazing manifestation exercise.' What we would like for people to do is, in the morning decide what they want and write it down. If they want to go to the gym, they want to go to the gym for 45 minutes, they want to have a lunch break where they get to enjoy themselves and not worry about work, they want to make five extra deals more than they usually do, they want to make $2,000 extra, whatever it is that they write down. They are going to write this down on a piece of paper. As they write these things down on a piece of paper, what they are going to do is to imagine their tasks as a ball. This ball in their hand is a solid ball of energy and this is now all the things that they want to get completed. Once they have filled their snow globe with light, once they have connected with their soul, all they must do is imagine that that ball which represents all of the things that they want to get done now comes in from the outside of the snow globe into their hands, and just imagine sitting with the ball in their hands until it dissolves. Once that ball dissolves, what has happened is, let us just say that someone says, 'I want to make $10,000 this month in extra income,' so they write that down. They imagine that desire as the ball. They pull this ball into their snow globe and* *they wait for it to dissolve. What is happening is anything that is keeping them from making the $10,000 is now being cut. As long as it's for their highest and best good. If it's not for their highest and best good, it won't happen. So this is the beauty of it, because we are using the Christ light, we are using God's love and commitment to His children to help them manifest whatever they want. Someone may have a block that says 'If I get rich I will lose all my money.' So maybe they have a cord attached to that belief that keeps them from making money. So when they pull this ball into their snow globe and it then dissolves, what is really happening is the guides, the angels, the higher self are cutting cords that are keeping them from making this money. Or maybe they have an ex-wife that they pay alimony to and their belief is, 'If I make more money, I will only have to give her more money.' So they'll cut the cord to the wife. So you don't need to know what the cords are. You don't need to know what they are about. Just pulling in this ball into their snow globe, letting it dissolve so that it is basically attuning them to what they want. Somebody wants to lose 45 pounds. 'I want to lose 45 pounds,' they need to be specific, 'I want to lose 45 pounds in five months.' They can pull that into their field, let it dissolve, and it's fine. They don't need to ever do it again. But write down the things that you pull into your snow globe so you can see when they come true. You don't have to revisit them for them to manifest but it is nice to revisit the list to see what has come into existence because it's easy to forget how powerful we are and when one sees all of their* *desires coming into their life, it is empowering. It's just like prayers; you don't need to say the same prayers over and over and over but if you acknowledge when they come to pass and say thank you, it is also empowering. Joe, if you want your fiancé to be over here in the United States, you can say, 'Me and my fiancé, in the United States,' and put it into a ball, and pull it into your field and let it dissolve, and all the cords that are blocking will be cut, and as long as it's for your highest and best good, it will happen. And you know that the universe is working on this. Many people can manifest the things that they want just by doing this exercise. And this is why we say that this exercise will make this book very, very popular, because it will lead into other books on manifestation using the snow globe.*

JOE: Thanks Jesus!!

PETER: There will be many books on how to use the snow globe to do different things. The Snow Globe will be very famous, very popular, and because of this all of your other books will be in demand as well. People will learn of all your other books and they will respect you guys, and you will start to heal the planet using a snow globe. How beautiful is that?"

JOE: Beautiful! Sounds good to me!!!

Epilogue

For a brief reference to who we as individuals are and where we came from, here is a short introductory chapter from *Answers Heaven Speaks*.

We have lived many lives. But we don't remember them. We, collectively, have heavenly-mandated amnesia. We don't remember starting our lives in Heaven before being born as humans. As in the Old Testament and Paul in the New Testament proclaim that God said (I am paraphrasing here), "I have known you before the filament of the earth and every hair on your head is counted" (Jeremiah 1:5 and Luke 12:7). We existed before we were born on earth. We came with personality and spirit, and we leave with personality and spirit. Our bodies, our vessels as they are called up there, remain here on earth, their usefulness completed.

Jesus also had amnesia. He says he figured out who he was when he was leaving his home at the age of nineteen but it wasn't until His baptism in the Jordan River by John the Baptist that he was truly able to connect with "the other side". After His baptism, Jesus began and concluded His planned mission on earth as a teacher and healer. On the other side, He was Christ, who built the universe and everything in it. On this side, He was a man who housed the soul of Christ. He no longer prayed to the Father in blind faith, for after his baptism, his angelic guides lifted the amnesia from his human mind and ego. His ministry commenced and then he died on a cross and was resurrected to rejoin his collective consciousness, his Higher Self which was none other than Christ, who is the Personality of God living with the first creation of Source/God, the Holy Spirit which lives within every facet of God's creation.

We come from our true home in Heaven. As odd as this may sound, Heaven is reality and earth is basically a Petrie dish where a duality of good and evil is allowed to co-exist. A planet with the duality of good and evil co-existing in the universe is rare, so despite the relatively young age of earth (their words); our collective consciousness leads us to believe that we are the center of the universe. Here is what the heavenly realms said about that (from my Higher Self):

There are many other realms, many other universes, many other dimensions and many other earths, some of which may not even know about our earth. Technically Joe, we do not agree that this earth is the center of the universe, but as a figure of speech, yes, there are many spiritual visitors who are watching and guiding us in order to help the earth become more like their planets. Because of this activity, our earth feels like it's the center of the universe. These visitors have watched as baby planets, like earth, developed and learned to sustain all forms of life, including humans. Unfortunately, they have watched these humanoids destroy their planets completely, so they need to recreate a new planet, like earth with animal life, plant life, oceans, rivers, and streams so that humans may be developed to the point, as in the planets that surround the

Pleiades, Arcturus, Andromeda, and Sirius, to evolve so that souls will be willing to incarnate into these humanoids. With the earth's duality, their souls like to incarnate on earth for the experience.

From the true home of everyone who has lived and died on earth, selected angels are watching this grand experiment that you and I are here to endure by design. We designed our lives in Heaven with the help of our spirit guides and the approval of our Souls all the way up to Christ. We also come from a Spiritual family in Heaven, a family that continues to incarnate together over time on earth in order to learn the lessons that our Souls predetermine us to experience. These are our soul mates, our soul family and soul group.

The only huge caveat is that *we are born into human animals with amnesia by design.* We don't remember where we came from. We are spirit and we have lived before.

Visit our website at
http://www.discoverintuition.com to
find more books written by Joe and
Marisa as well as other books written
by Marisa with Bill and Gayle
Gladstone.

Marisa teaches Intuition Development,
Spiritual development, and quantum
healing workshops at her Intuition
Development Center in Encinitas,
California where she works full time
with clients doing Intuitive Coaching,
Spiritual Counseling, and Channeling
advice and guidance for Entrepreneurs
who like her, have a desire to bring
light to the world!
For information on classes as well as
her web based classes on Intuition
University check out the site!

http://www.iammarisa.com
You can also find video lessons for
free by searching Marisa Moris in you
tube.

The Snow Globe

Made in the USA
San Bernardino, CA
10 December 2016